A History of Germs

THE FLU

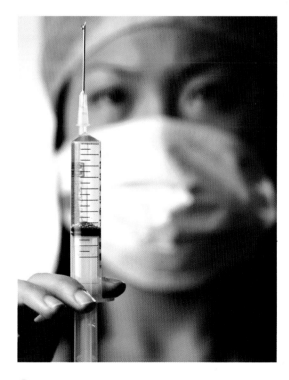

 By Jim Ollhoff

VISIT US AT

WWW.ABDOPUBLISHING.COM

Published by ABDO Publishing Company, 8000 West 78th Street, Suite 310, Edina, MN 55439. Copyright ©2010 by Abdo Consulting Group, Inc. International copyrights reserved in all countries. No part of this book may be reproduced in any form without written permission from the publisher. ABDO & Daughters™ is a trademark and logo of ABDO Publishing Company.

Printed in the United States.

PRINTED ON RECYCLED PAPER

Editor: John Hamilton
Graphic Design: Sue Hamilton
Cover Design: John Hamilton
Cover Photo: iStock
Interior Photos and Illustrations: AP-pgs 5, 7, 12, 23, 26, 27, & 29; Corbis-pg 21; Getty Images-pgs 15 & 17; iStockphoto-pgs 1 & 3; Jupiterimages-pgs 4, 6 & 28; Mary Evans Picture Library-pg 19; National Archives and Records Administration-pgs 16 & 31; National Library of Medicine-pgs 13 & 22; Naval Historical Center-pgs 14 & 22; Office of the Public Health Service Historian-pgs 9, 11, & 20; Photo Researchers-pgs 8, 10, & 25; United States Department of Health and Human Services-pgs 9, 11, 13, 16, 20, 22, & 31; and Wikimedia-pg 22.

Library of Congress Cataloging-in-Publication Data

Ollhoff, Jim, 1959-
  The flu / Jim Ollhoff.
     p. cm. – (A history of germs)
  Includes index.
  ISBN 978-1-60453-498-6
  1. Influenza–Juvenile literature. 2. Virus diseases–Juvenile literature. I. Title.

  QR201.I6O45 2010
  616.2'03–dc22

                              2008055063

CONTENTS

THE GREAT INFLUENZA

When people think about catching "the flu," they usually think of it as a very bad cold. The flu, or *influenza*, usually puts a person in bed for about a week, then leaves them feeling weak for a few more days. But after that, they feel better. Usually, influenza attacks the very young, the very old, or those who are already sick.

However, influenza comes in many different forms, or strains. In 1918, there was a terrible flu that spread across the entire world. It attacked people who were young and healthy.

It was often called the "Spanish flu" because many news reports of the epidemic first came from Spain. Some people called the epidemic "La Grippe," a French phrase that means "to seize." Others called it "The Great Influenza."

The flu usually puts sufferers in bed for about a week, then leaves them feeling weak for a few more days. However, the 1918 influenza strain was much more severe. It killed 50-100 million people worldwide.

The 1918 influenza was probably the deadliest pandemic in human history. About 500 million people were infected, almost one-third of the world's population at that time. Scientists and historians estimate that it killed between 50 and 100 million people across the globe. By comparison, World War I ended in 1918 with a death toll of about 20 million soldiers and civilians.

In the United States, the illness was fatal for about 2 percent of those who contracted the virus, killing about 700,000 people. In some areas of the world, the flu was fatal for 20 percent of the people who contracted it.

Cemeteries often have sections where all the headstones show that the people died in 1918.

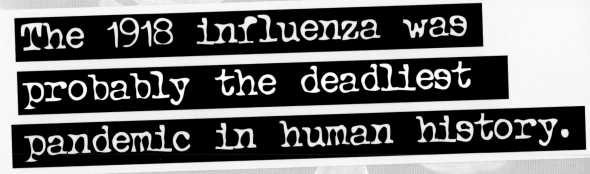

The 1918 influenza was probably the deadliest pandemic in human history.

HOW THE PANDEMIC STARTED

In 1918, the United States was a young country, ready to lead the world into the modern age. World War I had been going on since 1914. In 1917, the United States joined the war effort. Americans sang patriotic songs, heralding their arrival into the European war: "Send the word over there, the yanks are coming…"

America saw itself as an emerging, great nation. Scientists had already developed vaccines for smallpox, rabies, diphtheria, and other diseases. There was a belief that Americans could do anything.

Then, the Great Influenza hit.

A World War I soldier.

Today, scientists debate about where the influenza virus first began. Some scientists say China, others say France. The best research suggests that it began in southwest Kansas in January, 1918. There was an outbreak of influenza in Haskell County, Kansas. In late February, a few soldiers from the Army base at Fort Riley, Kansas, came home to Haskell County to visit family. After a few days, they returned to Fort Riley.

Then, on the morning of March 4, 1918, a soldier at Fort Riley went to the base hospital. He had a fever, sore throat, and headache. A minute later, another soldier came into the hospital. Then another. And another. By lunchtime, 100 soldiers had reported to the base hospital. By the end of the week, 500 soldiers were in hospital beds. Forty-eight of them died.

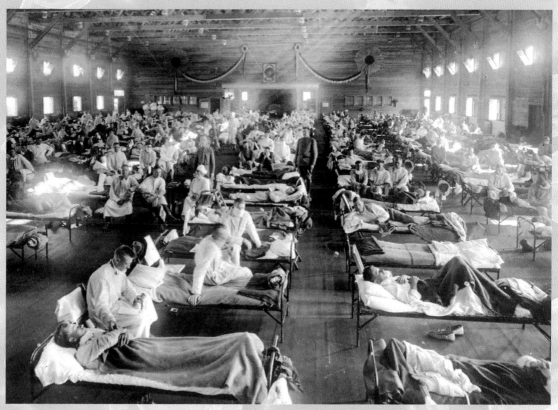

A 1918 photograph showing influenza victims crowded into an emergency hospital at Camp Funston, a subdivision of Fort Riley in Kansas.

There was a belief that Americans could do anything.

United States soldiers wore gauze masks to protect themselves from the flu.

   Soldiers from that base went to Europe, as well as other military bases around the country. Soldiers traveled on boats, where the close quarters made it easy for the virus to jump from one person to another. These soldiers would fight alongside soldiers from different countries. Soldiers would go home and infect their families. Then, the neighborhood would be infected, and then whole cities. By September 1918, the influenza was rampant in the military and spreading into cities. The virus traveled quickly and easily into every part of the world.

   People wanted to support the war effort, so they participated in parades and rallies. In large groups, the virus spread quickly. People crowded into rooms to hear the latest news about the war. The virus spread. In many cities, people lived close together, where the virus spread terrifyingly fast.

Nothing like this had ever happened before, so many people didn't know how to respond. Officials in some cities reassured people that the influenza couldn't happen in their town. Some officials denied that there was a problem. Most people were so concerned about the war that they simply couldn't be bothered with the influenza news.

By October, entire cities were infected. Hospitals were full. The supply of caskets for the dead had run out. Hospitals stacked the dead in hallways leading toward the morgue. The Great Influenza would soon become a full-blown worldwide pandemic.

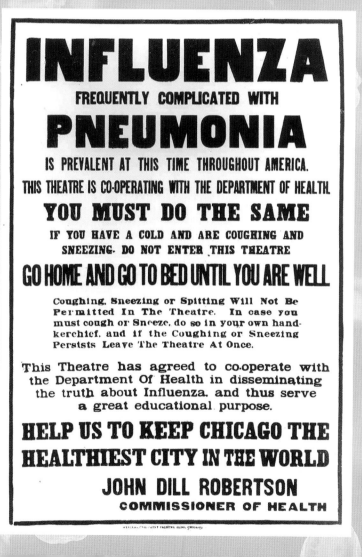

A 1918 influenza poster placed in American theaters. Health professionals tried desperately to stop the pandemic that was sweeping the world.

WHAT IS INFLUENZA?

The 1918 influenza, like all influenza, was caused by a virus. A virus is a kind of germ, a microscopic agent that inserts its DNA into another cell. It essentially hijacks the cell, taking it over and forcing the cell to make more viruses. Influenza attacks the respiratory system, including the nose, throat, and lungs.

The 1918 influenza virus probably started as an avian flu, a virus that only affected birds. If it had stayed that way, it wouldn't have been harmful to humans. But then it mutated, which means that its makeup changed. Germs are in a constant state of mutation. In January 1918, it mutated and became dangerous to people.

A microscope view of influenza virus particles, or virions.

Adults and children dutifully wore gauze masks to protect themselves from the flu. Unfortunately, the masks did little good against the influenza virus.

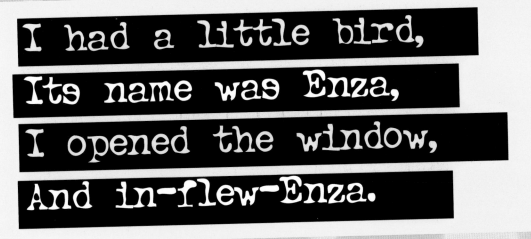

I had a little bird,
Its name was Enza,
I opened the window,
And in-flew-Enza.

—American Skipping Rhyme, 1918

William H. Sardo, Jr., was six years old in 1918 when he got the flu. As a survivor of the epidemic, he is likely still immune to the influenza infection.

People who survived the influenza infection developed an immunity. A human body's immune system changes constantly. When the immune system fights off a virus, it "remembers" that virus and can later fight it more effectively. People with immunity to a particular germ usually don't get infected again. Doctors found that children who survived the 1918 influenza were still immune to it 70 years later.

There are many different forms of influenza. The Greek philosopher Hippocrates wrote about an influenza epidemic in 412 BC. There have been outbreaks of deadly influenza all through history. However, scientists think that the 1918 outbreak was one of the deadliest influenza outbreaks ever.

One of the things that made the 1918 flu so deadly was that it had several ways to kill its victims. The most common way was a secondary infection. The virus killed off the protective lining of cells in the lungs. This protective lining is a defense against bacteria. When the virus killed off that protection, the lungs were easy prey for deadly bacteria. Since antibiotics had not been invented yet, people had little defense against the bacteria.

Another way that the 1918 influenza virus killed its victims was a process called a cytokine storm. Cytokines are a vital part of the body's immune system, but the influenza virus made them overactive. The cytokines would not turn off, and so the immune system overreacted to the virus. Fluid built up in the tissues, cutting off vital body functions. In this way, people were killed by their own immune system. This is one of the reasons why the young and healthy were hardest hit by the influenza. Those with the strongest immune system were most vulnerable when their immune systems went into overdrive.

When it came to treating influenza patients, doctors, nurses, and druggists were at a loss. The young and healthy were the hardest hit.

Germs can't fly on their own. However, because the influenza virus settled in the lungs, coughing made a lot of the germs airborne. They floated through the air on tiny droplets from people's coughs, sneezes, or even just from talking. When people inhaled the virus, it lodged in the soft membranes of their nose or lungs. Once there, the virus began to do its work.

The Liberty Loan parade took place in September 1918, in Philadelphia, Pennsylvania. About 200,000 people attended the event. Just days later, hundreds of cases of influenza were reported. A single infected person who coughed could infect everyone nearby. Millions learned this too late. More Americans died from influenza than died in World War I.

A single infected person who coughed could infect everyone in a crowded room. Because of the war effort, there were lots of places with crowded rooms. The influenza virus had an easy time spreading.

The first flu symptoms included a sore throat, coughing, and headache. Dizziness and body aches were common. High fevers lasted a few days. Sometimes, the symptoms struck quickly and severely. A person could be walking down the street and be suddenly struck with weakness and dizziness, and then collapse right on the street.

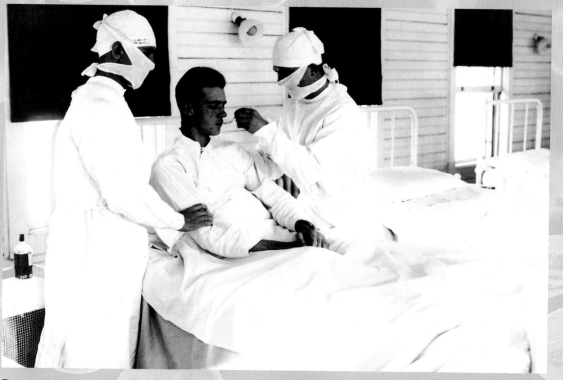

Doctors treat a 1918 influenza patient at the U.S. Naval Hospital in New Orleans. As the disease progressed, people sometimes coughed up their own blood.

As the virus raged inside the body, the insides of the nose and mouth became red and inflamed. Sneezing and bloody noses were common. Sometimes, the fever got so bad that people started hallucinating. If the disease continued, the lungs began to fill up with blood and fluid, and people would cough up their own blood.

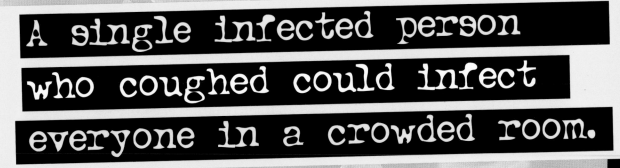

A single infected person who coughed could infect everyone in a crowded room.

GOOD AND DESPERATE TREATMENTS

Nurses and doctors attempted, often unsuccessfully, to protect themselves from influenza.

The terrible flu pandemic raged through the last half of 1918. Parents, officials, and doctors tried a variety of treatments. Some were based on science, but others were pure desperation.

Doctors didn't know what was making people sick. Their optical microscopes couldn't see viruses. Viruses had been discovered 20 years earlier, but doctors didn't understand them very well. Most thought victims were suffering from a bacterial infection. Scientists kept trying to find a vaccine, but kept failing. Their technology to find the source of the disease was very limited. Doctors had no effective antibiotics, and no antiviral medication. The best they could do was try to keep the victims' fevers from getting too high.

Policemen in Seattle, Washington, wore masks in the belief that these would protect them from influenza. The masks provided no real protection.

Doctors knew that the illness was transmitted through the air by coughing and sneezing. Many cities quickly passed laws requiring people to wear face masks whenever they went outside. However, they used the wrong kind of fabric for the masks. The mesh of the fabric was too thin and loose to stop the influenza virus. It was like trying to stop a mosquito with a chain-link fence. The masks were mostly useless as a defense against the virus.

Masks were mostly useless as a defense against the virus.

Adults, such as this miner, as well as young children, were instructed to gargle with various solutions. Gargling was supposed to wash the mouth clean of the flu, but it was an ineffective treatment.

Since they didn't realize that a virus was the cause of the pandemic, people began to invent reasons why the disease had struck. Some claimed that German soldiers planted the influenza in this country. Since the United States was at war with Germany, it seemed logical to blame the Germans. Other people blamed the poison gasses used in Europe during the war. Some blamed the fumes from all the exploding bombs in the war. Some people blamed the dust from coal, or fleas. Some people even blamed dirty dishwater.

Why catch their Influenza?

YOU need not! Just carry Formamint with you and suck these delicious tablets whenever you are in danger of being infected by other people.

"Suck at least four or five a day"—so says Dr. Hopkirk in his standard work "Influenza"—for "in Formamint we possess the best means of preventing the infective processes which, if neglected, may lead to serious complications."

Seeing that such complications often lead to Pneumonia, Bronchitis, and other dangerous diseases, it is surely worth while to protect yourself by this safe, certain, and inexpensive means. Protect the children, too, for their delicate little organisms are very exposed to germ-attack, especially during school-epidemics. Be careful, however, not to confuse Formamint with so-called formalin tablets, but see that it bears the name of the sole manufacturers: Genatosan, Limited (British Purchasers of Sanatogen Co.), 12, Chenies Street, London, W.C. 1. (Chairman: The Viscountess Rhondda.)

"Attack the germs before they attack you!"

Though genuine Formamint is scarce your chemist can still obtain it for you at the pre-war price—2/2 per bottle. Order it to-day.

Formamint
THE GERM KILLING THROAT TABLET

Formamint advertised itself as "Your Safe Shield against Infectious Illness." People also turned to traditional cold remedies in hopes of preventing the flu.

People had many ideas for preventing and treating influenza. Some believed they should chew their food very carefully, or avoid tight clothes. Some people gargled with strange chemicals to try to kill the germs in their throat. Some parents made their children eat onions, thinking that onions had curative powers. Other folk remedies included holding garlic in the mouth or eating sugar laced with drops of kerosene. While these remedies had no effect on the influenza virus, people wanted to believe that doing something—anything—was better than just sitting waiting to die.

THE VIRUS STOPS

By September and October of 1918, many cities banned gatherings of people. Schools were closed, churches were empty. Parks and playgrounds were deserted. People were afraid to talk to each other for fear of getting influenza.

The sick were quarantined. Hospitals overflowed. Many sick people lay on hospital floors because all the regular beds were taken. Many doctors and nurses had been sent to Europe to help during World War I, so there were fewer medical staff than usual. This put extra strain on hospitals.

By the fall of 1918, hospitals were overflowing with patients.

New York street cleaners wore masks. "Better be ridiculous then dead" was the view of one official. Unfortunately, the masks did not help. By October 1918, the streets of many cities were deserted. People were afraid to go out.

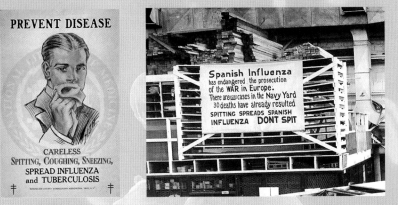

To help stop the spread of influenza, signs were posted warning people to cover their mouths when they coughed, and not to spit.

In some cities, carts came at night to collect the bodies of the dead. Large cities used steam shovels to dig mass graves. Public signs reminded people to cover their mouths when they coughed. Fear gripped the country.

Then, in early November 1918, the influenza pandemic began to decline. The virus had wreaked havoc on almost every part of the world. Only a few islands and other isolated areas escaped the influenza onslaught. The virus had infected much of humanity. But then the deaths began to slow. No action by the medical community decreased the infection rate. The disease slowed on its own.

When an epidemic hits a huge part of the population, nearly everyone gets infected. Some people have a natural immunity. Some people die. Those who get sick but survive develop immunity and can't be infected again. That's what happened with the 1918 influenza virus.

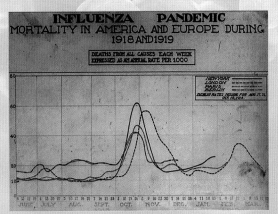

Just as deaths had hit their peak, suddenly in November 1918, the pandemic began to decline. The disease slowed on its own.

Masks forgotten, people cheer the end of World War I on Armistice Day, November 11, 1918, outside of the White House in Washington, D.C. The flu pandemic was on the decline.

There were no more people to infect. The virus had simply run its course. One doctor of the time put it bluntly. He said, "The virus had run out of people to kill."

On November 11, 1918, the fighting of World War I ended. There was worldwide celebration. Cities had parades, and people, wearing masks, danced in the streets.

Some doctors were celebrating, too. They realized that the influenza epidemic was decreasing. In San Francisco, people were allowed to take off their masks on November 21. Some people still got sick, even into December, but at a much lower rate. By early 1919, the influenza virus was mostly a terrible memory.

"The virus had run out of people to kill."

STUDYING THE 1918 INFLUENZA VIRUS

Scientists are very interested in the 1918 influenza virus. They try to understand why it was so deadly. One problem is that doctors and scientists in 1918 didn't leave very good records. They had limited technology and weren't able to give scientific data. Even when noting the cause of death, doctors in 1918 sometimes wrote "pneumonia," or "fever," or "coughing." Sometimes, doctors misdiagnosed the disease entirely. That makes it frustrating for today's doctors to do research into why the 1918 virus was so deadly.

But, there have been a few chances for today's doctors to get good information. In 2008, doctors analyzed lung tissue from 58 soldiers who had died in 1918. These tissue samples had been preserved in blocks of wax for 70 years. Today's doctors were able to find important information about the virus.

In 1996, scientists traveled to the Norwegian island of Spitsbergen. Buried in the permanently frozen ground were six people who died from the 1918 virus. After getting permission from relatives, the remains of these people were exhumed and studied. The cold weather kept the remains frozen and well preserved, so doctors were able to examine the virus and run tests on how and why it was so deadly. Doctors also studied the remains of a 1918 influenza victim who was buried in the frozen tundra of northern Alaska. These studies bring a greater understanding of the virus—and how to stop the next influenza epidemic.

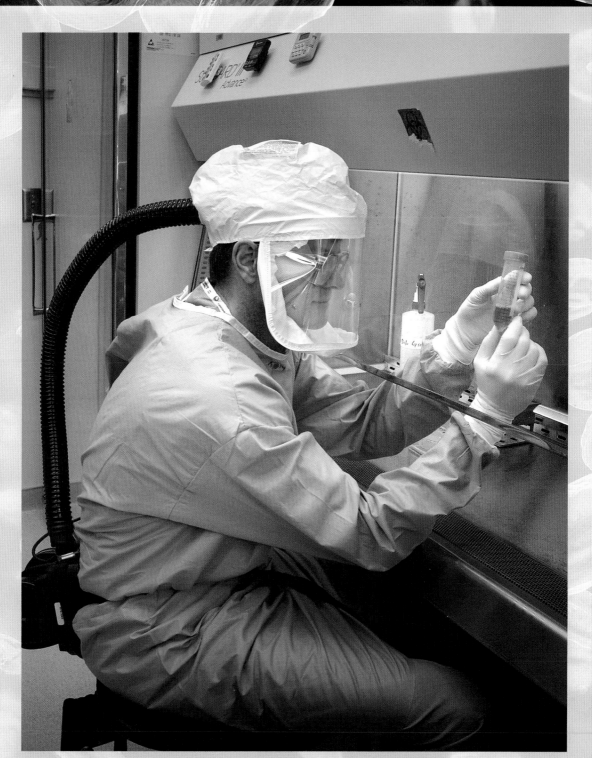

In a secure room, a scientist wearing protective gear examines a sample of the influenza virus strain that caused the 1918 Spanish flu pandemic.

INFLUENZA TODAY

Each year in the United States, 200,000 people are hospitalized with "normal" influenza, and 36,000 people die. Most victims are infants or the elderly, or were sick before the flu virus struck them. New strains of influenza emerge each year. Scientists make educated guesses about which strain will be the biggest health threat. Then, they manufacture vaccines for that strain.

In 1957, the "Asian flu" killed approximately two million people. In 1968, the "Hong Kong flu" killed 700,000. In 1976, there was a scare about the "Swine flu." Health officials were concerned about the Swine flu because it was similar to the 1918 virus. However, the virus never became a major health threat.

The first shipment of Asian flu vaccine arrived by plane in the United States in August 1957.

New strains of influenza emerge each year.

Recently, scientists warned of the spread of avian influenza, or "bird flu." Normally found in birds, the virus mutated and "jumped species," infecting humans in the late 1990s. This version of flu has a high mortality rate—it is fatal for about 60 percent of the people who contract it. Luckily, the virus is not spread from human to human—so far. Scientists at the World Health Organization (WHO) and the Centers for Disease Control and Prevention (CDC) continue to keep a close watch on the situation.

In 1998, a member of the Hong Kong Agriculture and Fisheries Department medical staff, dressed in special sanitary gear, prepares to take blood samples from a batch of live chickens from China. Hong Kong and other countries had banned the poultry from being imported after several people died from H5N1 influenza, also known as "bird flu."

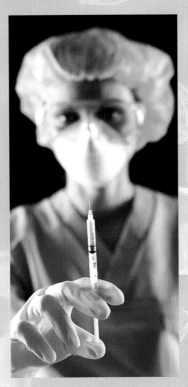

Flu vaccines are created every year.

Will another influenza virus become a health threat? Almost certainly. However, scientists can respond quicker than ever to make new vaccines and save lives. Antiviral medications slow and sometimes stop viruses. Antibiotics can kill bacterial infections.

Still, germs are changing all the time. Vaccines will only protect people from one strain of influenza, not all strains. Can we act quickly when a new strain of influenza emerges?

In 2009, a flu epidemic erupted in Mexico. Scientists named it the H1N1 flu. Since it was originally a virus found in pigs, it is often called "swine flu." It spread very quickly in Mexico, and many people died. Then it spread to other countries, including the United States. Because this was a new and unexpected virus, the old flu vaccines didn't work. Immediately, scientists started developing a new vaccine. In the meantime, health authorities put out many alerts, and recommended that schools temporarily close when someone was diagnosed with the flu.

However, while the H1N1 virus spread quickly, fewer deaths were reported outside Mexico. At first, scientists weren't sure why it was lethal in one place, and mild in other places. The WHO and CDC will monitor the spread and severity of the H1N1 virus for several years.

After the first H1N1 scare in early 2009, some people accused the WHO and CDC of overreacting. However, doctors at these institutions can't predict how a virus will behave. They have to do their best to protect people. If they make a mistake, it's always better to err on the side of caution.

A mother and daughter wait to see a doctor in Mexico City in April 2009. Fearing a major flu outbreak, officials in Mexico warned citizens to stay home, urged businesses to close, and stopped public events.

GLOSSARY

CDC
The Centers for Disease Control and Prevention (CDC) is a United States agency that studies and protects public health. One of its jobs is to monitor the world for influenza outbreaks.

DNA
DNA is short for the scientific term Deoxyribonucleic Acid. In living things, DNA is the material inside the center of every cell that forms genes. This material is inherited from an individual's parents.

EPIDEMIC
A sudden emergence of a new disease.

IMMUNITY
The immune system in humans "remembers" when a virus or bacteria attack after first exposure. From then on, the immune system can kill the virus quickly.

MUTATION
Viruses and bacteria mutate, or change, over time. This presents a problem for humans who developed immunity to the old virus, but not the new mutated version. The 1918 virus may have originally infected only birds, but it mutated so that it became infectious to humans as well.

PANDEMIC

When an epidemic emerges over a large area, such as a continent or even worldwide. The 1918 influenza virus was a pandemic.

QUARANTINE

The practice of separating sick people from healthy people. This is important when diseases are contagious.

WHO

The World Health Organization (WHO) is an agency of the United Nations. One of its tasks is to monitor outbreaks of influenza through its Global Influenza Surveillance Network. Countries report to the WHO any outbreaks, and the WHO distributes influenza information across the world.

In 1918, when mail carriers came down with influenza, even the mail was delayed.

INDEX